The Golden Girls

MAD LIBS®

by Douglas Yacka and Francesco Sedita

Mad Libs
An Imprint of Penguin Random House

MAD LIBS
Penguin Young Readers Group
An Imprint of Penguin Random House LLC

Mad Libs format copyright © 2017 by Penguin Random House LLC.
All rights reserved.

Concept created by Roger Price & Leonard Stern

© Touchstone

Published by Mad Libs,
an imprint of Penguin Random House LLC,
345 Hudson Street, New York, New York 10014.
Printed in the USA.

ISBN 9780451534033
5 7 9 10 8 6

MAD LIBS®

INSTRUCTIONS

MAD LIBS® is a game for people who don't like games!
It can be played by one, two, three, four, or forty.

• RIDICULOUSLY SIMPLE DIRECTIONS

In this tablet you will find stories containing blank spaces where words
are left out. One player, the READER, selects one of these stories. The
READER does not tell anyone what the story is about. Instead, he/she asks
the other players, the WRITERS, to give him/her words. These words are
used to fill in the blank spaces in the story.

• TO PLAY

The READER asks each WRITER in turn to call out a word—an adjective or
a noun or whatever the space calls for—and uses them to fill in the blank
spaces in the story. The result is a MAD LIBS® game.

When the READER then reads the completed MAD LIBS® game to the other
players, they will discover that they have written a story that is fantastic,
screamingly funny, shocking, silly, crazy, or just plain dumb—depending
upon which words each WRITER called out.

• EXAMPLE (*Before* and *After*)

"_____!" he said _____
　　　　　EXCLAMATION　　　　　　　　　　　　　　　ADVERB

as he jumped into his convertible _____ and
　　　　　　　　　　　　　　　　　　　　　　　　NOUN

drove off with his _____ wife.
　　　　　　　　　　ADJECTIVE

"_____**OUCH**_____!" he said _____**STUPIDLY**_____
　　　　　EXCLAMATION　　　　　　　　　　　　　　　ADVERB

as he jumped into his convertible _____**CAT**_____ and
　　　　　　　　　　　　　　　　　　　　　　NOUN

drove off with his _____**BRAVE**_____ wife.
　　　　　　　　　　ADJECTIVE

In case you have forgotten what adjectives, adverbs, nouns, and verbs are, here is a quick review:

An ADJECTIVE describes something or somebody. *Lumpy, soft, ugly, messy,* and *short* are adjectives.

An ADVERB tells how something is done. It modifies a verb and usually ends in "ly." *Modestly, stupidly, greedily,* and *carefully* are adverbs.

A NOUN is the name of a person, place, or thing. *Sidewalk, umbrella, bridle, bathtub,* and *nose* are nouns.

A VERB is an action word. *Run, pitch, jump,* and *swim* are verbs. Put the verbs in past tense if the directions say PAST TENSE. *Ran, pitched, jumped,* and *swam* are verbs in the past tense.

When we ask for A PLACE, we mean any sort of place: a country or city (*Spain, Cleveland*) or a room (*bathroom, kitchen*).

An EXCLAMATION or SILLY WORD is any sort of funny sound, gasp, grunt, or outcry, like *Wow!, Ouch!, Whomp!, Ick!,* and *Gadzooks!*

When we ask for specific words, like a NUMBER, a COLOR, an ANIMAL, or a PART OF THE BODY, we mean a word that is one of those things, like *seven, blue, horse,* or *head.*

When we ask for a PLURAL, it means more than one. For example, *cat* pluralized is *cats.*

MAD LIBS® is fun to play with friends, but you can also play it by yourself! To begin with, DO NOT look at the story on the page below. Fill in the blanks on this page with the words called for. Then, using the words you have selected, fill in the blank spaces in the story.

Now you've created your own hilarious MAD LIBS® game!

WELCOME TO SHADY PINES!

ADJECTIVE _____

ADJECTIVE _____

PLURAL NOUN _____

OCCUPATION (PLURAL) _____

ADJECTIVE _____

A PLACE _____

NOUN _____

ADJECTIVE _____

NOUN _____

ADJECTIVE _____

VERB ENDING IN "ING" _____

ADJECTIVE _____

NUMBER _____

TYPE OF FOOD _____

NOUN _____

ADJECTIVE _____

VERB _____

NOUN _____

MAD LIBS®
WELCOME TO SHADY PINES!

Are you looking for a place for your _____ mother to live out
                                        ADJECTIVE

her remaining years? Shady Pines Retirement Home provides the most

comfortable and _____ environment you will find, and is sure
                    ADJECTIVE

to please even the most particular of _____. Our
                                          PLURAL NOUN

_____ and nurses are the most _____ you will
OCCUPATION (PLURAL)   ADJECTIVE

find in (the) _____. They provide round-the-_____
                A PLACE   NOUN

care for all of our _____ residents. Each room is furnished
                        ADJECTIVE

with a/an _____-size bed, _____ lighting, and hot
              NOUN   ADJECTIVE

and cold _____ water. _____ meals are served
            VERB ENDING IN "ING"   ADJECTIVE

_____ times a day, including our famous _____
   NUMBER   TYPE OF FOOD

parmesan and chicken pot _____. We even have a/an
                              NOUN

_____ garden, where our residents can _____ in the
   ADJECTIVE   VERB

fresh air. Shady Pines guarantees your mother a home surrounded by

_____ and tranquility.
   NOUN

From THE GOLDEN GIRLS MAD LIBS® • © Touchstone.
Published in 2017 by Mad Libs, an imprint of Penguin Random House LLC.

MAD LIBS® is fun to play with friends, but you can also play it by yourself! To begin with, DO NOT look at the story on the page below. Fill in the blanks on this page with the words called for. Then, using the words you have selected, fill in the blank spaces in the story.

Now you've created your own hilarious MAD LIBS® game!

ROSE'S SPERHEOVEN KRISPIES

ADJECTIVE _____

NOUN _____

NOUN _____

ADVERB _____

TYPE OF LIQUID _____

PLURAL NOUN _____

ADJECTIVE _____

TYPE OF FOOD _____

ADJECTIVE _____

ADJECTIVE _____

NUMBER _____

PART OF THE BODY _____

ADJECTIVE _____

TYPE OF FOOD _____

ADJECTIVE _____

NOUN _____

ADJECTIVE _____

MAD LIBS®
ROSE'S SPERHEOVEN KRISPIES

Can't sleep? Perhaps it's time to make a/an _____ batch of

                                        ADJECTIVE

Sperheoven Krispies, direct from Rose's _____! An ancient

                                  NOUN

Scandinavian midnight _____, perfect for the hungriest of

                              NOUN

Vikings after a night of pillaging. They go _____ with a hot

                                    ADVERB

cup of _____! Now, baker be warned, the smell of these

         TYPE OF LIQUID

_____ can be worse than a dirty garbage can full of

  PLURAL NOUN

_____ fish heads and moldy _____. When they're

  ADJECTIVE   TYPE OF FOOD

baking in your oven and you can't stand the _____ smell of

                                      ADJECTIVE

them anymore, you know they're done! Carefully remove the tray from

the oven and let these _____ delicacies cool for _____

                        ADJECTIVE   NUMBER

minutes. Then you hold your _____ with one hand and pop

                              PART OF THE BODY

a Krispie in your mouth with the other! They taste simply

_____! Like cheesecake, chocolate _____, and

  ADJECTIVE   TYPE OF FOOD

_____ strawberries! These Saint Olaf classics are sure to put

  ADJECTIVE

you to sleep with a/an _____ on your face and a/an

                        NOUN

_____ stomach!

  ADJECTIVE

From THE GOLDEN GIRLS MAD LIBS® • © Touchstone.
Published in 2017 by Mad Libs, an imprint of Penguin Random House LLC.

MAD LIBS® is fun to play with friends, but you can also play it by yourself! To begin with, DO NOT look at the story on the page below. Fill in the blanks on this page with the words called for. Then, using the words you have selected, fill in the blank spaces in the story.

Now you've created your own hilarious MAD LIBS® game!

OUT ON THE LANAI

PART OF THE BODY _____

ADJECTIVE _____

OCCUPATION _____

VERB _____

ANIMAL _____

TYPE OF FOOD _____

NOUN _____

ADJECTIVE _____

NOUN _____

NOUN _____

NOUN _____

NOUN _____

MAD LIBS®

OUT ON THE LANAI

You would think that the Girls' lanai would be the perfect place to relax

and clear your _____, but it seems that something
                      PART OF THE BODY

_____ is always happening out there! Like when . . .
ADJECTIVE

- Blanche hires a stripper dressed as a/an _____ to
                                              OCCUPATION

  _____ at Dorothy's bridal shower.
  VERB

- A man in a/an _____ costume parachutes down,
                  ANIMAL

  thinking he is at the _____ Bowl.
                         TYPE OF FOOD

- Rose sees a/an _____ in the night sky and thinks it's a
                  NOUN

  UFO!

- Dorothy and Miles get swept away in the _____
                                            ADJECTIVE

  moonlight and share a forbidden _____.
                                   NOUN

- Sophia puts a Sicilian _____ on the neighbor after his
                          NOUN

  _____ crashes onto their _____.
  NOUN   NOUN

From THE GOLDEN GIRLS MAD LIBS® • © Touchstone.
Published in 2017 by Mad Libs, an imprint of Penguin Random House LLC.

MAD LIBS® is fun to play with friends, but you can also play it by yourself! To begin with, DO NOT look at the story on the page below. Fill in the blanks on this page with the words called for. Then, using the words you have selected, fill in the blank spaces in the story.

Now you've created your own hilarious MAD LIBS® game!

TONIGHT AT THE RUSTY ANCHOR

SILLY WORD (PLURAL) _____

PLURAL NOUN _____

NOUN _____

TYPE OF LIQUID _____

ADJECTIVE _____

ADJECTIVE _____

VERB ENDING IN "ING" _____

NOUN _____

VERB _____

ADJECTIVE _____

TYPE OF FOOD _____

NOUN _____

VERB _____

MAD LIBS
TONIGHT AT THE RUSTY ANCHOR

- **Musical Monday:** Start the week right with two-for-one Mai

  _____ as we sing the classics from your favorite
  <u>SILLY WORD (PLURAL)</u>

  Broadway _____.
  <u>PLURAL NOUN</u>

- **Tiptoe Through Tuesday:** There's nothing better than an

  ice-cold _____ and songs from an era gone by.
  <u>NOUN</u>

- **Wet and Wild Wednesday:** Two-for-one shots of

  _____! Show us what the good Lord gave you in
  <u>TYPE OF LIQUID</u>

  your _____ white T-shirt.
  <u>ADJECTIVE</u>

- **Thirsty Thursday:** Join some of our nation's _____
  <u>ADJECTIVE</u>

  heroes—astronauts—as they take time off _____
  <u>VERB ENDING IN "ING"</u>

  on earth, and rehydrate with our Tang-tinis.

- **Flip Cup Friday:** It's game night at the Rusty _____.
  <u>NOUN</u>

  The more you _____, the more _____ we look!
  <u>VERB</u> <u>ADJECTIVE</u>

- **Saturday Sizzler:** We're grilling _____ out on the patio.
  <u>TYPE OF FOOD</u>

  Start early with a bite and leave late with a/an _____!
  <u>NOUN</u>

- **Sing It Out Sunday:** Tonight, ladies _____ for free as
  <u>VERB</u>

  long as they come with a song to sing!

From THE GOLDEN GIRLS MAD LIBS® • © Touchstone.
Published in 2017 by Mad Libs, an imprint of Penguin Random House LLC.

MAD LIBS® is fun to play with friends, but you can also play it by yourself! To begin with, DO NOT look at the story on the page below. Fill in the blanks on this page with the words called for. Then, using the words you have selected, fill in the blank spaces in the story.

Now you've created your own hilarious MAD LIBS® game!

THANK YOU FOR BEING A/AN _____
NOUN

ADJECTIVE _____

ADJECTIVE _____

VERB _____

ANIMAL _____

VERB _____

VERB _____

VERB _____

ADJECTIVE _____

VERB _____

VERB _____

VERB _____

ADJECTIVE _____

ANIMAL _____

MAD LIBS®
THANK YOU FOR BEING A/AN _____
NOUN

The Girls explain what it means to be a true friend:

Blanche: In the South, we are known for being _____, loyal,
ADJECTIVE

and _____. Above all else, you never _____ your
ADJECTIVE   VERB

friend's boyfriend, no matter how much you like him!

Sophia: In Sicily, sometimes the only friend I had was a/an

_____. And let me tell you something, they stink! They stink at
ANIMAL

being your friend, and they don't know how to _____ pinochle!
VERB

Rose: In Saint Olaf, we learned to _____ friends from a very
VERB

early age. It was said that in years with a lot of rain, your friendships

were like true silver—they would _____ if you didn't care for
VERB

them properly!

Dorothy: Growing up in _____ Brooklyn, we had one
ADJECTIVE

credo—_____ all, _____ a few, and learn to
VERB   VERB

_____ your own canoe. But there are only a few friends you
VERB

need in this world. And I'm _____ to have found mine.
ADJECTIVE

Sophia: That's nice, pussy-_____. Too bad you all had to wait
ANIMAL

until you were almost dead to find them!

From THE GOLDEN GIRLS MAD LIBS® • © Touchstone.
Published in 2017 by Mad Libs, an imprint of Penguin Random House LLC.

MAD LIBS® is fun to play with friends, but you can also play it by yourself! To begin with, DO NOT look at the story on the page below. Fill in the blanks on this page with the words called for. Then, using the words you have selected, fill in the blank spaces in the story.

Now you've created your own hilarious MAD LIBS® game!

MY STUPID
EX-HUSBAND, STAN

ADJECTIVE _____

PLURAL NOUN _____

ANIMAL (PLURAL) _____

PLURAL NOUN _____

ADJECTIVE _____

PART OF THE BODY _____

SILLY WORD _____

NUMBER _____

ADJECTIVE _____

NOUN _____

NOUN _____

ADJECTIVE _____

ANIMAL _____

VERB (PAST TENSE) _____

VERB _____

NOUN _____

MAD LIBS®
MY STUPID
EX-HUSBAND, STAN

Let me tell you about the most _____ idiot I know, who
_{ADJECTIVE}

happens to be my ex-husband and the father of our _____,
_{PLURAL NOUN}

Stanley Zbornak. Stan makes his living selling novelties like rubber

_____, plastic animal poop, and whoopee _____.
_{ANIMAL (PLURAL)}   _{PLURAL NOUN}

Let's just say that he is not the most _____ businessman.
_{ADJECTIVE}

When it comes to money, Stan doesn't know his _____ from
_{PART OF THE BODY}

his elbow. In fact, we almost got thrown in jail because the big

_____ didn't file our taxes for _____ years! Oh, and did
_{SILLY WORD}   _{NUMBER}

I mention that he left me after forty _____ years for a/an
_{ADJECTIVE}

_____ half his age? Stan thinks of himself as a ladies' man but
_{NOUN}

he is about as charming as a/an _____, and as smart as one,
_{NOUN}

too. But the most _____ thing about Stan is his toupee. It
_{ADJECTIVE}

looks like a/an _____ crawled onto his head and
_{ANIMAL}

_____. Every time I see him, I want to _____
_{VERB (PAST TENSE)}   _{VERB}

it off and flush it down the _____!
_{NOUN}

From THE GOLDEN GIRLS MAD LIBS® • © Touchstone.
Published in 2017 by Mad Libs, an imprint of Penguin Random House LLC.

MAD LIBS® is fun to play with friends, but you can also play it by yourself! To begin with, DO NOT look at the story on the page below. Fill in the blanks on this page with the words called for. Then, using the words you have selected, fill in the blank spaces in the story.

Now you've created your own hilarious MAD LIBS® game!

REMEMBER THAT ONE? PART 1

NOUN _____

TYPE OF FOOD _____

NOUN _____

NOUN _____

NOUN _____

VERB _____

VERB _____

VERB _____

VERB (PAST TENSE) _____

Rose: "My _____ always used to say, 'The older you get, the
_{NOUN}

better you get, unless you're a/an _____.'"
_{TYPE OF FOOD}

Rose: "They say you can lead a herring to _____, but you
_{NOUN}

have to walk really fast or he'll die."

Sophia: "We could use the Sicilian method. We burn down the house,

collect the fire insurance money, and move to a beautiful beachside

_____ in California."
_{NOUN}

Dorothy: "Why should I deny being in denial? I never said I was in denial.

You are the one who said I was in _____, and don't you deny it!"
_{NOUN}

Sophia: "_____ your seatbelt, slut puppy. This ain't gonna be
_{VERB}

no cakewalk!"

Dorothy: "Blanche, have you heard of the latest campaigns? 'Join the

navy, see the world, _____ with Blanche Devereaux?' 'Join the
_{VERB}

army, be all you can be . . . _____ with Blanche Devereaux?'
_{VERB}

'The marines are looking for a few good men who have not

_____ with Blanche Devereaux!'"
_{VERB (PAST TENSE)}

From THE GOLDEN GIRLS MAD LIBS® • © Touchstone.
Published in 2017 by Mad Libs, an imprint of Penguin Random House LLC.

MAD LIBS® is fun to play with friends, but you can also play it by yourself! To begin with, DO NOT look at the story on the page below. Fill in the blanks on this page with the words called for. Then, using the words you have selected, fill in the blank spaces in the story.

Now you've created your own hilarious MAD LIBS® game!

HOW TO RENOVATE A BATHROOM

ADJECTIVE _____

ADJECTIVE _____

ADJECTIVE _____

NOUN _____

TYPE OF LIQUID _____

COLOR _____

NOUN _____

ADJECTIVE _____

ADJECTIVE _____

ADJECTIVE _____

MAD LIBS®
HOW TO RENOVATE
A BATHROOM

Sometimes, a girl has to do things for herself. Here are a few

_____ tips on how to renovate a bathroom:
   ADJECTIVE

- Don't let that _____ plumber tell you that it's going
                    ADJECTIVE

  to be a hard job. Listen to what he has to say, but remember that

  you have survived many difficult things in your life, like your

  _____ husband, Stan, running off with a stewardess
      ADJECTIVE

  who promised him a/an _____ in Hawaii.
                             NOUN

- Check to make sure that all the water pressure is off, otherwise

  there may be an explosion of _____ in your face.
                                TYPE OF LIQUID

- Decide what your color scheme should be. Palm Tree

  _____ or maybe even _____ Pink.
     COLOR   NOUN

- Choose your fixtures. A faucet is one of the most important

  things to make your powder room feel _____.
                                         ADJECTIVE

- Make sure that everything you ordered is up to your

  _____ standards.
     ADJECTIVE

Now, get to work! That powder room will be _____ in no
                                            ADJECTIVE

time!

From THE GOLDEN GIRLS MAD LIBS® • © Touchstone.
Published in 2017 by Mad Libs, an imprint of Penguin Random House LLC.

MAD LIBS® is fun to play with friends, but you can also play it by yourself! To begin with, DO NOT look at the story on the page below. Fill in the blanks on this page with the words called for. Then, using the words you have selected, fill in the blank spaces in the story.

Now you've created your own hilarious MAD LIBS® game!

DATING OVER SIXTY

ADJECTIVE _____

VERB ENDING IN "ING" _____

FOREIGN COUNTRY _____

VERB ENDING IN "ING" _____

OCCUPATION _____

VERB _____

NOUN _____

NOUN _____

VERB ENDING IN "ING" _____

PART OF THE BODY _____

PLURAL NOUN _____

PART OF THE BODY _____

CELEBRITY (MALE) _____

CELEBRITY (MALE) _____

ADJECTIVE _____

NOUN _____

MAD☺LIBS®

DATING OVER SIXTY

It's not easy for a Golden Girl to find _____ love. Here is
                                          ADJECTIVE

some advice for _____ Mr. Right.
                 VERB ENDING IN "ING"

- If he flies you to _____ on the first date, things are
                      FOREIGN COUNTRY

  definitely _____ too fast.
              VERB ENDING IN "ING"

- Just because he tells you he's a/an _____ doesn't mean
                                       OCCUPATION

  he knows how to _____.
                   VERB

- If he spends the night in your _____, make sure he
                                  NOUN

  doesn't leave his dentures on your _____.
                                      NOUN

- He should always ask before _____ you on the
                               VERB ENDING IN "ING"

  lips or holding your _____.
                       PART OF THE BODY

- Check to see that he still has all his _____ and that
                                         PLURAL NOUN

  he can reach down to touch his _____.
                                 PART OF THE BODY

- Even if he has the charm of _____ and the good looks
                              CELEBRITY (MALE)

  of _____, be cautious. He could turn out to be a/an
      CELEBRITY (MALE)

  _____ _____ in the end.
   ADJECTIVE   NOUN

From THE GOLDEN GIRLS MAD LIBS® • © Touchstone.
Published in 2017 by Mad Libs, an imprint of Penguin Random House LLC.

MAD LIBS® is fun to play with friends, but you can also play it by yourself! To begin with, DO NOT look at the story on the page below. Fill in the blanks on this page with the words called for. Then, using the words you have selected, fill in the blank spaces in the story.

Now you've created your own hilarious MAD LIBS® game!

PICTURE IT—SICILY, 1912

A PLACE _____

ADJECTIVE _____

NOUN _____

ADVERB _____

ADJECTIVE _____

VERB _____

ADJECTIVE _____

ANIMAL _____

TYPE OF FOOD _____

ADJECTIVE _____

PART OF THE BODY (PLURAL) _____

PLURAL NOUN _____

TYPE OF FOOD _____

ADJECTIVE _____

VERB _____

NUMBER _____

MAD LIBS

PICTURE IT—SICILY, 1912

Picture it—(the) _____, 1912. A/An _____ peasant
A PLACE   ADJECTIVE

girl meets a/an _____ and they fall _____ in love.
NOUN   ADVERB

Her _____ parents disapprove, however, and she decides to
ADJECTIVE

_____ away from the village. For months, she travels the
VERB

_____ countryside, riding a/an _____ and living
ADJECTIVE   ANIMAL

only on _____. Finally, she gathers up enough courage to
TYPE OF FOOD

return to her _____ village. Worried that she will never be
ADJECTIVE

accepted again, she is greeted with open _____. She
PART OF THE BODY (PLURAL)

and her parents do the traditional dance of the _____ and
PLURAL NOUN

celebrate with a feast of _____. Everyone is _____
TYPE OF FOOD   ADJECTIVE

with joy. The point is this: No matter how far away you _____,
VERB

you have to remember to cook the spaghetti sauce for _____
NUMBER

hours!

From THE GOLDEN GIRLS MAD LIBS® • © Touchstone.
Published in 2017 by Mad Libs, an imprint of Penguin Random House LLC.

MAD LIBS® is fun to play with friends, but you can also play it by yourself! To begin with, DO NOT look at the story on the page below. Fill in the blanks on this page with the words called for. Then, using the words you have selected, fill in the blank spaces in the story.

Now you've created your own hilarious MAD LIBS® game!

PAGE ONE FROM BLANCHE'S MANUSCRIPT

ADJECTIVE _____

FIRST NAME (FEMALE) _____

ADJECTIVE _____

PERSON IN ROOM (MALE) _____

VERB (PAST TENSE) _____

PART OF THE BODY (PLURAL) _____

VERB (PAST TENSE) _____

FIRST NAME (FEMALE) _____

VERB _____

VERB ENDING IN "ING" _____

COLOR _____

PART OF THE BODY _____

ADJECTIVE _____

MAD LIBS
PAGE ONE FROM
BLANCHE'S MANUSCRIPT

'Twas a dark and _____ night. _____ Dubois

ADJECTIVE   FIRST NAME (FEMALE)

stood in the dappling moonlight, the air moist and _____

ADJECTIVE

around her. She knew her daddy would be cross with her if he knew

that she was waiting to meet _____, one of the finest

PERSON IN ROOM (MALE)

young men to ever be _____ in the South. She waited

VERB (PAST TENSE)

in anticipation, smoothing down her dress with her dainty

_____. Just then she heard a noise in the distance.

PART OF THE BODY (PLURAL)

Her heart fluttered and her bosom _____. Could this

VERB (PAST TENSE)

finally be happening? "_____, is that you?" he asked.

FIRST NAME (FEMALE)

"Why, yes. Yes, it is. I am here for you, waiting for you to take me, right

here, in the middle of the field we used to _____ on." He

VERB

stepped forward, the moonlight _____ in his big

VERB ENDING IN "ING"

_____ eyes. She felt a chill down her _____. "I must

COLOR   PART OF THE BODY

first tell you something, my love. There's something you don't know

about me. That no one knows about me. I'm . . . I'm _____."

ADJECTIVE

From THE GOLDEN GIRLS MAD LIBS® • © Touchstone.
Published in 2017 by Mad Libs, an imprint of Penguin Random House LLC.

MAD LIBS® is fun to play with friends, but you can also play it by yourself! To begin with, DO NOT look at the story on the page below. Fill in the blanks on this page with the words called for. Then, using the words you have selected, fill in the blank spaces in the story.

Now you've created your own hilarious MAD LIBS® game!

ROSE NYLUND, REPORTER

NOUN _____

ADJECTIVE _____

ADJECTIVE _____

PLURAL NOUN _____

TYPE OF FOOD _____

NUMBER _____

TYPE OF LIQUID _____

ADJECTIVE _____

VERB ENDING IN "ING" _____

OCCUPATION _____

VERB ENDING IN "ING" _____

TYPE OF FOOD _____

ADJECTIVE _____

VERB _____

COLOR _____

ADJECTIVE _____

ADJECTIVE _____

MAD LIBS®

ROSE NYLUND, REPORTER

This is Rose Nylund, investigative _____, reporting to you
                                                  NOUN

live from Miami's most _____ supermarket, where someone
                                       ADJECTIVE

has been stealing groceries! This _____ situation began last
                                           ADJECTIVE

week when one of the store's _____ noted that
                                        PLURAL NOUN

_____ was missing from aisle _____. The next day, a
TYPE OF FOOD   NUMBER

gallon of _____ disappeared. Since then, all sorts of
                TYPE OF LIQUID

_____ items have gone _____. The store's
ADJECTIVE   VERB ENDING IN "ING"

_____ was _____ near the deli counter
OCCUPATION   VERB ENDING IN "ING"

when he noticed that the thief had taken every single _____
                                             TYPE OF FOOD

in the building. The suspect is believed to be a short, _____,
                                           ADJECTIVE

elderly Italian woman, who has been known to _____ in the
                                        VERB

store before. No one has been able to catch her _____-handed.
                                          COLOR

What is even more _____ is that an unusually large number
                           ADJECTIVE

of groceries have been showing up in my kitchen at home. I guess we

will never know who this _____ thief is for sure!
                               ADJECTIVE

From THE GOLDEN GIRLS MAD LIBS® • © Touchstone.
Published in 2017 by Mad Libs, an imprint of Penguin Random House LLC.

MAD LIBS® is fun to play with friends, but you can also play it by yourself! To begin with, DO NOT look at the story on the page below. Fill in the blanks on this page with the words called for. Then, using the words you have selected, fill in the blank spaces in the story.

Now you've created your own hilarious MAD LIBS® game!

THERE'S A CHEESECAKE IN THE FRIDGE

ADJECTIVE _____

VERB _____

TYPE OF LIQUID _____

NOUN _____

PLURAL NOUN _____

NOUN _____

NOUN _____

NOUN _____

NOUN _____

TYPE OF LIQUID _____

NOUN _____

NOUN _____

PLURAL NOUN _____

VERB _____

PLURAL NOUN _____

When you can't get a/an _____ night's sleep, sometimes the

ADJECTIVE

only thing to do is walk to the kitchen and _____. Here are

VERB

some of the best late-night sleep remedies:

- There's always **warm** _____. It just takes a moment

TYPE OF LIQUID

  to heat up and it feels so good going down.

- If you're dieting, make **a/an** _____ **parfait**. Throw

NOUN

  some _____ on top of plain yogurt with a little

PLURAL NOUN

  granola, or a secret sprinkle of _____ chips!

NOUN

- There's always **ice cream** in the freezer. You can grab a/an
  _____ and go to town on some Rocky _____

NOUN *NOUN*

  or, if you feel adventurous, a/an _____ split, complete with

NOUN

  _____ and a/an _____ on top!

TYPE OF LIQUID *NOUN*

- And finally, there's the mother of all late-night snacks—

  the cheesecake. It's perfect for a late-night chat with a/an

  _____ of coffee. And it's best when shared with friends,

NOUN

  where you can tell each other _____, make each other

PLURAL NOUN

  _____, and celebrate life's little _____!

VERB *PLURAL NOUN*

MAD LIBS® is fun to play with friends, but you can also play it by yourself! To begin with, DO NOT look at the story on the page below. Fill in the blanks on this page with the words called for. Then, using the words you have selected, fill in the blank spaces in the story.

Now you've created your own hilarious MAD LIBS® game!

ROOMMATE WANTED

NUMBER _____

ADJECTIVE _____

PLURAL NOUN _____

COLOR _____

COLOR _____

NOUN _____

NOUN _____

VERB _____

TYPE OF LIQUID _____

VERB _____

PLURAL NOUN _____

NOUN _____

TYPE OF FOOD _____

VERB _____

ADJECTIVE _____

MAD LIBS®

ROOMMATE WANTED

An attractive, sassy, single girl is looking for _____ roommates.
                                                    NUMBER

I live in a/an _____ home right here in Miami with some of
                ADJECTIVE

the most beautiful decor. If you love wicker _____, accents
                                              PLURAL NOUN

of tropical _____ and pastel _____, and a lanai so
              COLOR   COLOR

you can bake your beautiful body in the _____, this is the
                                          NOUN

place for you! I am a/an _____ at the museum, where I
                          NOUN

_____ quite hard. But I also love to have a good time. Monday
  VERB

is my favorite happy hour at the Rusty Anchor, where the boys all buy

me glasses of _____ and let me _____ my favorite
                TYPE OF LIQUID   VERB

show tunes at the piano. I am looking for girls who want to enjoy

themselves. Definitely no cats and absolutely no _____.
                                                   PLURAL NOUN

Someone who knows her way around the _____ and who can
                                        NOUN

whip up a sinfully rich _____ moves to the front of the line!
                          TYPE OF FOOD

And most importantly, you must be able to _____ the rent on
                                            VERB

time and know how to mix up a/an _____ mint julep!
                                   ADJECTIVE

MAD LIBS® is fun to play with friends, but you can also play it by yourself! To begin with, DO NOT look at the story on the page below. Fill in the blanks on this page with the words called for. Then, using the words you have selected, fill in the blank spaces in the story.

Now you've created your own hilarious MAD LIBS® game!

THE TROUBLE WITH SIBLINGS

PART OF THE BODY _____

NOUN _____

ADJECTIVE _____

NOUN _____

VERB ENDING IN "ING" _____

ADJECTIVE _____

VERB (PAST TENSE) _____

ADVERB _____

NOUN _____

NOUN _____

ADJECTIVE _____

NOUN _____

NUMBER _____

ADJECTIVE _____

NOUN _____

PART OF THE BODY (PLURAL) _____

MAD LIBS®

THE TROUBLE WITH SIBLINGS

No matter how old you are, brothers and sisters can be a real

_____-ache. Dorothy doesn't like her sister, Gloria, because
PART OF THE BODY

she is a snooty _____ and thinks she is too _____ for
                      NOUN   ADJECTIVE

everyone. To make matters worse, Dorothy caught Gloria and her

ex-_____, Stan, _____ in her bed. Blanche
        NOUN   VERB ENDING IN "ING"

and her sister Virginia often fight over which of them is more

_____ to behold and who has _____ more
    ADJECTIVE   VERB (PAST TENSE)

men. But the two sisters _____ make up when Virginia gets
                                ADVERB

sick and asks for Blanche's _____ to save her _____.
                                   NOUN   NOUN

Blanche also doesn't approve of her brother Clayton when he tells her

he's _____, even after he brings home the new _____
         ADJECTIVE   NOUN

he is in love with! Sophia and her sister have a/an _____-year
                                                         NUMBER

feud where they put _____ Sicilian curses on each other like,
                         ADJECTIVE

"May your marinara sauce never cling to your _____!" or
                                                    NOUN

"May your _____ sag so low that you need a belt to
             PART OF THE BODY (PLURAL)

keep them up!"

From THE GOLDEN GIRLS MAD LIBS® • © Touchstone.
Published in 2017 by Mad Libs, an imprint of Penguin Random House LLC.

MAD LIBS® is fun to play with friends, but you can also play it by yourself! To begin with, DO NOT look at the story on the page below. Fill in the blanks on this page with the words called for. Then, using the words you have selected, fill in the blank spaces in the story.

Now you've created your own hilarious MAD LIBS® game!

OLD-WORLD WISDOM

FIRST NAME (FEMALE) _____

SAME FIRST NAME (FEMALE) _____

NOUN _____

PART OF THE BODY _____

ADJECTIVE _____

FIRST NAME (MALE) _____

TYPE OF FOOD _____

ADJECTIVE _____

NOUN _____

SAME FIRST NAME (FEMALE) _____

OCCUPATION _____

ARTICLE OF CLOTHING (PLURAL) _____

Listen, let me tell you a story about my sister Angela's best friend

_____ Dellaterlizzi. See, _____ never
FIRST NAME (FEMALE)   SAME FIRST NAME (FEMALE)

thought she would find true _____ and happiness in the
                                      NOUN

foothills of Sicily. Every morning, she would tell me and Angela about

how big her _____ was and that she was certain no man could
            PART OF THE BODY

ever fill it. But when she was seventeen, she met a/an _____
                                                            ADJECTIVE

young man named _____ DeRobertis-Milano of the
                  FIRST NAME (MALE)

famous DeRobertis-Milano family. They made some of the best

_____ in all of Sicily. And even though they fell in love, his
TYPE OF FOOD

father said that unless she could learn how to make the _____
                                                              ADJECTIVE

family recipe of zeppole, his son could not marry her. Well, she worked

for months to learn it. The secret was that the dough had to fry in the

_____ for just three minutes. But sadly, she was never able to
NOUN

make the recipe correctly. As it turns out, she never married. The last

time I spoke to Angela, _____ had run off with a/an
                          SAME FIRST NAME (FEMALE)

_____ and she had even taken to wearing men's
OCCUPATION

_____.
ARTICLE OF CLOTHING (PLURAL)

From THE GOLDEN GIRLS MAD LIBS® • © Touchstone.
Published in 2017 by Mad Libs, an imprint of Penguin Random House LLC.

MAD LIBS® is fun to play with friends, but you can also play it by yourself! To begin with, DO NOT look at the story on the page below. Fill in the blanks on this page with the words called for. Then, using the words you have selected, fill in the blank spaces in the story.

Now you've created your own hilarious MAD LIBS® game!

A NOTE FROM MRS. ZBORNAK

PERSON IN ROOM _____

NOUN _____

ADVERB _____

NUMBER _____

OCCUPATION _____

PERSON IN ROOM _____

ARTICLE OF CLOTHING (PLURAL) _____

PART OF THE BODY _____

NOUN _____

PERSON IN ROOM _____

PART OF THE BODY _____

VERB _____

SILLY WORD _____

Dear Parent,

I am writing to you today about your lovely child, _____.
                                                    PERSON IN ROOM
While I do understand that every parent believes his or her child is

God's _____ to the world, I must tell you that in this case, you
         NOUN
are _____ wrong. I have been teaching for _____ years,
    ADVERB   NUMBER
and while I am only a substitute _____, the behavior I have
                                  OCCUPATION
seen from little _____ is atrocious. Your child has pulled their
                 PERSON IN ROOM
_____ down and has wiggled their
ARTICLE OF CLOTHING (PLURAL)
_____ in the middle of my English lessons numerous times.
PART OF THE BODY
However, I believe that we can make a difference here. I ask that you

agree to meet with me as a family once a week. _____ is of the
                                                NOUN
essence here. Little _____ seems to be getting worse. This
                     PERSON IN ROOM
morning, I found them drawing a/an _____ in the
                                    PART OF THE BODY
bathroom with a marker! Please call me at your earliest convenience

so we can _____ this problem immediately.
          VERB
Sincerely yours,

Dorothy _____
        SILLY WORD

MAD LIBS® is fun to play with friends, but you can also play it by yourself! To begin with, DO NOT look at the story on the page below. Fill in the blanks on this page with the words called for. Then, using the words you have selected, fill in the blank spaces in the story.

Now you've created your own hilarious MAD LIBS® game!

THAT'S ENTERTAINMENT!

NOUN _____

A PLACE _____

ADJECTIVE _____

NUMBER _____

SILLY WORD _____

CELEBRITY _____

ARTICLE OF CLOTHING _____

EXCLAMATION _____

PLURAL NOUN _____

COLOR _____

NOUN _____

PLURAL NOUN _____

TYPE OF LIQUID _____

PLURAL NOUN _____

CELEBRITY (MALE) _____

CELEBRITY (FEMALE) _____

NOUN _____

MAD LIBS®

THAT'S ENTERTAINMENT!

Bet you didn't know that Miami is one of the premier cities to visit if

you are a/an _____ of the arts, second only to (the)
                NOUN

_____. One _____ gallery downtown recently
  A PLACE   ADJECTIVE

unveiled an exhibit featuring _____ paintings by Pablo
                                  NUMBER

_____. Another featured a sculpture of _____
  SILLY WORD   CELEBRITY

wearing nothing but a/an _____, causing a passerby
                          ARTICLE OF CLOTHING

to gasp and shout _____! The city's symphony performs
                    EXCLAMATION

_____ for special occasions like Miami's _____
  PLURAL NOUN   COLOR

Bowl Parade and _____ Day fireworks. All of the city's
                   NOUN

_____ turn out for the Food and _____
  PLURAL NOUN   TYPE OF LIQUID

Festival, a showcase of culinary _____. And let's not forget
                                  PLURAL NOUN

the theater! Where else can you catch a matinee of Mr. _____
                                                        CELEBRITY (MALE)

playing Hamlet or _____ singing her heart out in *The*
                    CELEBRITY (FEMALE)

_____ *and I?*
  NOUN

MAD LIBS® is fun to play with friends, but you can also play it by yourself! To begin with, DO NOT look at the story on the page below. Fill in the blanks on this page with the words called for. Then, using the words you have selected, fill in the blank spaces in the story.

Now you've created your own hilarious MAD LIBS® game!

BLANCHE'S SOUTHERN-FRIED SAYINGS

PLURAL NOUN _____

PLURAL NOUN _____

NOUN _____

PERSON IN ROOM _____

VERB _____

A PLACE _____

ADJECTIVE _____

ADJECTIVE _____

VERB _____

NOUN _____

NOUN _____

ADJECTIVE _____

PERSON IN ROOM (MALE) _____

PERSON IN ROOM (MALE) _____

VERB ENDING IN "ING" _____

MAD LIBS®
BLANCHE'S
SOUTHERN-FRIED SAYINGS

Blanche certainly has a way with words, especially when she speaks

about _____!
     PLURAL NOUN

- I do believe your sweet _____ could charm the
                  PLURAL NOUN

  _____ right off the honeysuckle!
  NOUN

- I swear that, _____ as my witness, I will never
            PERSON IN ROOM

  _____ another man. In (the) _____. On a
    VERB   A PLACE

  Saturday. Unless he's _____ . . . and drives a nice car.
               ADJECTIVE

- Like Big Daddy always said about me, I have hair as

  _____ as the dew on a field of sunflowers, eyes that
  ADJECTIVE

  _____ as blue as the Mississippi, and the prettiest smile
  VERB

  this side of the Mason-Dixon _____.
                         NOUN

- Oh, I'll never forget it! That night under the dogwood

  _____, the air _____ with perfume, and me
  NOUN   ADJECTIVE

  with _____. Or was it _____?
  PERSON IN ROOM (MALE)   PERSON IN ROOM (MALE)

- I'm from the South! _____ is part of my
                    VERB ENDING IN "ING"

  heritage!

MAD LIBS® is fun to play with friends, but you can also play it by yourself! To begin with, DO NOT look at the story on the page below. Fill in the blanks on this page with the words called for. Then, using the words you have selected, fill in the blank spaces in the story.

Now you've created your own hilarious MAD LIBS® game!

REMEMBER THAT ONE, PART 2

VERB _____

VERB _____

ADJECTIVE _____

PART OF THE BODY _____

PLURAL NOUN _____

NOUN _____

NOUN _____

NOUN _____

Dorothy: "Rose, I know this is a long shot, but did you _____
VERB

much acid in the sixties?"

Sophia: "When I _____ my hearing aid up to ten, I can hear
VERB

a canary break wind in Lauderdale!"

Dorothy: "You'll have to excuse my mother. She suffered a slight stroke

a few years ago, which rendered her totally _____."
ADJECTIVE

Sophia: "There's just something I don't like about him. I can't put my

_____ on it, but if I did, I'd have to wash it."
PART OF THE BODY

Rose: "Tell me, is it possible to love two _____ at the same
PLURAL NOUN

time?"

Blanche: "Set the scene; have we been drinking?"

Dorothy: "Step on a/an _____, break your mother's back. It
NOUN

doesn't work—I know."

Blanche: "Of course God exists! Just look at the beautiful

_____, the majestic trees. God created man and gave him
NOUN

a/an _____, and a mind, and thighs that could crack walnuts."
NOUN

MAD LIBS® is fun to play with friends, but you can also play it by yourself! To begin with, DO NOT look at the story on the page below. Fill in the blanks on this page with the words called for. Then, using the words you have selected, fill in the blank spaces in the story.

Now you've created your own hilarious MAD LIBS® game!

THE FINAL EPISODE

NUMBER _____

PLURAL NOUN _____

PLURAL NOUN _____

NOUN _____

NOUN _____

VERB _____

COLOR _____

PLURAL NOUN _____

VERB _____

VERB _____

NOUN _____

NOUN _____

NOUN _____

ADJECTIVE _____

PERSON IN ROOM _____

ADJECTIVE _____

PLURAL NOUN _____

NOUN _____

MAD LIBS®

THE FINAL EPISODE

In the _____-part series finale of *The Golden Girls*,
NUMBER

_____ are revealed, truths are uncovered, and
PLURAL NOUN

_____ are changed forever! Has Dorothy found her one
PLURAL NOUN

true _____? Will she actually walk down the _____?
NOUN   NOUN

What will she _____ to her wedding? A/An _____
VERB   COLOR

dress, even though Sophia said only _____ wear white
PLURAL NOUN

twice? And what about Stanley? Maybe he will _____ down the
VERB

aisle after Dorothy, screaming, "I _____ you! I always have!
VERB

Don't make this _____!" Will Blanche bless this _____
NOUN   NOUN

between her best friend and her _____? And is she destined to
NOUN

be _____ forever? And will Rose return to her hometown,
ADJECTIVE

Saint _____? Will she finally stop asking _____
PERSON IN ROOM   ADJECTIVE

questions? And don't forget about Sophia! Will she be forced to return

to Shady _____ and eat chicken a la _____ for her
PLURAL NOUN   NOUN

final days?